ID0422877

A Special Gift

WITH LOVE TO

Stephanie Anderson

From

Dana Burns (Best Friend)

Copyright © 1995 by Christian Art. All rights reserved

Published in South Africa by Christian Art Publishers
P.O. Box 1599, Vereeniging, South Africa

Coedition arranged by Christian Art, South Africa

Design & Photographic Styling: Lizette Jonker

Photography:
Mariam Gillan (cover, floral frames, p 9*, 21, 29*, 37*)
Lizette Jonker (p 13, 17, 25, 33, 41, 45)
* Courtesy of *Essentials*

Scriptural texts from:
• The Living Bible, Coverdale House Publishers Ltd.
• Special Edition Good News Bible, © Bible Society, London, 1979

ISBN 0-8007-7166-4

Printed in Singapore

WITH LOVE TO ...

A Special Friend

Fleming H. Revell
A Division of Baker Book House
Grand Rapids, Michigan 49516

Friends always show their love. What are brothers for if not to share trouble?

~ Proverbs 17:17 ~

Some friendships do not last, but some friends are more loyal than brothers.

~ Proverbs 18:24 ~

Friend – a person known well to another and regarded with liking, affection and loyalty.

~ Collins English Dictionary ~

*Anybody can sympathize
with the sufferings of a friend, but
it requires a very fine nature to
sympathize with a friend's success.*

~ Oscar Wilde ~

Those friends thou hast,
and their adoption tried,
Grapple them to thy
soul with hoops of steel;
But do not dull thy palm
with entertainment
Of each new-hatch'd,
unfledg'd comrade.

~ William Shakespeare ~

11

Friendship with oneself is all-important because without it one cannot be friends with anyone else in the world.

~ Eleanor Roosevelt ~

12

If you judge people, you have no time to love them.

~ Mother Teresa ~

I will speak ill of no man, and speak all the good I know of everybody.

~ Benjamin Franklin ~

14

*M*isfortune shows those
who are not really friends.

~ Aristotle ~

*T*rue friendship is a plant of slow
growth, and must undergo and
withstand the shocks of adversity
before it is entitled to the appellation.

~ George Washington ~

*K*eep your friendships in repair.

~ Ralph Waldo Emerson ~

*T*he bird a nest,
the spider a web,
man friendship.

~ William Blake ~

*F*riendship is love with wings.

~ Anonymous ~

16

*N*ever injure a friend, even in jest.

~ Cicero ~

*B*e slow to fall into friendship;
but when thou art in,
continue firm and constant.

~ Socrates ~

18

When true friends meet in adverse hour;
'Tis like a sunbeam through a shower.
A watery way an instant seen,
The darkly closing clouds between.

~ Sir Walter Scott ~

*... no man is useless
while he has a friend.*

~ Robert Louis Stevenson ~

*Think where man's glory
most begins and ends,
And say my glory was
I had such friends.*

~ William Yeats ~

20

*An honest answer is a
sign of true friendship.*

~ Proverbs 24:26 ~

*A friend means well,
even when he hurts you.
But when an enemy puts
his arm round your
shoulder – watch out!*

~ Proverbs 27:6 ~

22

One loyal friend is worth ten thousand relatives.

~ Euripides ~

The proper office of a friend is to side with you when you are in the wrong. Nearly anybody will side with you when you are in the right.

~ Mark Twain ~

23

Irue friends don't spend time gazing into each other's eyes. They may show great tenderness toward each other, but they face in the same direction – toward common projects, interests, goals – above all, toward a common Lord.

~ C.S. Lewis ~

24

*Your friend is your field which you sow
with love and reap with thanksgiving.*

~ Anonymous ~

*True happiness consists not
in the multitude of friends,
but in their worth and choice.*

~ Samuel Johnson ~

26

I can never think of promoting my
convenience at the expense of a
friend's interest and inclination.

~ George Washington ~

G rief can take care of itself, but to
get the full value of a joy you must
have somebody to divide it with.

~ Mark Twain ~

27

Thus nature has no love for
solitude, and always leans,
as it were, on some support; and
the sweetest support is found
in the most intimate friendship.

~ Cicero ~

Advice is like snow; the softer it falls, the longer it dwells upon, and the deeper it sinks into the mind.

~ Samuel Taylor Coleridge ~

The best mirror is an old friend.

~ George Herbert ~

*With every friend I love who has
been taken into the brown bosom
of the earth a part of me has been
buried there; but their contribution
to my being of happiness, strength
and understanding remains to
sustain me in an altered world.*

~ Helen Keller ~

*The death of a friend is
equivalent to the loss of a limb.*

~ German Proverb ~

31

*W*hat is a friend? A
single soul in two bodies.

~ Aristotle ~

A friend is a person with
whom I may be sincere.
Before him I may think aloud.

~ Ralph Waldo Emerson ~

32

My friends are my estate.
Forgive me then the avarice
to hoard them. They tell me
those who were poor early
have different views of gold.
I don't know how that is. God
is not so wary as we, else
He would give us no friends,
lest we forget Him.

~ Emily Dickinson ~

Don't walk in front of me
I may not follow
Don't walk behind me
I may not lead
Walk beside me
And just be my friend.

~ Albert Camus ~

The friendship that can cease has never been real.

~ Saint Jerome ~

I count myself in nothing else so happy As in a soul rememb'ring my good friends.

~ William Shakespeare ~

36

I find friendship to be like wine, raw
when new, ripened with age, the true
old man's milk and restorative cordial.

~ Thomas Jefferson ~

S ir, more than kisses, letters, mingle souls;
For, thus friends absent speak.

~ John Donne ~

38

Too late we learn, a
man must hold his friend
Unjudged, accepted,
trusted to the end.

~ John Boyle O'Reilly ~

Friends have all things in common.

~ Plato ~

Without friends no one would choose to live, though he had all other goods.

~ Aristotle ~

My best friend is the one who brings out the best in me.

~ Henry Ford ~

40

The greatest love a person can have for his friends is to give his life for them.

~ John 15:13 ~

What sunshine is to flowers, smiles are to humanity. They are but trifles, to be sure but, scattered along life's pathway, the good they do is inconceivable.

~ Joseph Addison ~

42

No soul is desolate as long as there is a human being for whom it can feel trust and reverence.

~ George Eliot ~

It is a sweet thing, friendship, a dear balm, A happy and auspicious bird of calm ...

~ Shelley ~

43

*The only reward of virtue
is virtue; the only way to have
a friend is to be one.*

~ Ralph Waldo Emerson ~

*A friend in need
is a friend indeed.*

~ Latin Proverb ~

44